Phrasebook for the Pleiades

Phrasebook for the Pleiades

poems

Lorraine Doran

Cider Press Review
San Diego

PHRASEBOOK FOR THE PLEIADES
Copyright © 2014 by Lorraine Doran. All rights reserved. No part of this book may be reproduced or utilized in any manner whatsoever without written permission, except in the case of brief quotations embodied in critical articles and reviews. Inquiries should be addressed to:

>   Cider Press Review
>   PO BOX 33384
>   San Diego, CA, 92163 USA
>   CIDERPRESSREVIEW.COM

First edition
10 9 8 7 6 5 4 3 2 1 0

ISBN: 978-1-930781-13-9
Library of Congress Control Number: 2013943554

Cover art: *Gramma Blue*, by Tristan Hutchinson
Cover design by Caron Andregg

ABOUT THE CIDER PRESS REVIEW BOOK AWARD:

The annual Cider Press Review Editors Prize offers a $1,500 prize, publication, and 25 author's copies of a book-length collection of poetry. For complete guidelines and information, visit CIDERPRESSREVIEW.COM/BOOKAWARD.

Printed in the United States of America
at Thomson-Shore, in Dexter, MI.

For Irene Doran

CONTENTS

Acknowledgments — vii

Promenade — 3

ONE

Satellite Photos of Our Former Homes — 7
    (Legend) — 7
    (28 Adamson) — 8
    (229 H_____) — 9
    (200 Mt. Pleasant) — 10
    (45 Plaza) — 11
Postcard (Tyniec) — 12
Take — 13
Watching the Girl — 15
The Lifespan of Birds — 16
September — 18
A series of disconnected events — 19
It is quite possible (after all) — 20
On Balance — 21

TWO

The Horse Letters (one) — 25
The Horse Letters (two) — 26
Postcard (Los Angeles) — 27
Poem Written on the Moon — 28
Insomnia — 29

Snow Machines, Astor Place	30
The Horse Letters (three)	31
Ventriloquism	32
The Horse Letters (four)	34
Postcard (Krakow)	35
Cygnus	36
Nocturne: Shelter Island	37
Bathymetry of Lake Michigan	38
The Whole Is Greater	40
Organic machinery	42

THREE

Only one element of each kind	45
Billie Holiday	46
Nancy Spungen	47
The Color and the Shape	48
Eve	49
Map of Trees	50
Lazarus	51
If the Soul Has a Shape	52
Diane Arbus	54
Soteriology	56
The Naming of Things	58
Elliott Smith	59

FOUR

…And We Shall All Be Clean	63
The Damascus Encyclopedia	64
(Circle)	64
(Tadpole)	65
(Ice)	66
(Salt)	67
(Script)	68
(Field)	69
Postcard (from a train)	70
Letter to Colin Concerning the Birds of Poland	71
Postcard (Montreal)	73
Postcard (Prague)	74
Bronze with Rabbits	75
Chicken	76
Leaving Barcelona	78
Notes	81

ACKNOWLEDGMENTS

I am grateful to the editors of the following journals, in which these poems first appeared, sometimes in a different form:

American Poetry Journal: "Promenade" and "Postcard (Tyniec)"
Arbella: "Elliott Smith"
Barn Owl Review: "229 H___," "200 Mt. Pleasant," "Ice," and "Field"
Big Hammer: "…And We Shall All Be Clean"
Cider Press Review: "Nocturne: Shelter Island"
FIELD: "The Horse Letters (four)"

"Promenade" was reprinted in *Verse Daily*. "Diane Arbus" and "Map of Trees" were published in *What's Your Exit: A Literary Detour Through New Jersey*. "The Whole Is Greater" was published in *Viva La Difference*, an anthology of poems inspired by the Peter Saul painting. "Organic machinery" first appeared etched into glass in Derek Ayres' sculpture *Fountain Pen*.

Thank you Gray Jacobik and everyone at *Cider Press Review* for believing in this book.

I am grateful to the Anderson Center for Interdisciplinary Studies for the time and space in which several of these poems were written.

Many thanks to my teachers and fellow poets – Ciaran Berry, Colin Cheney, Frankie Drayus, Amy Farranto, Eamon Grennan, Pat Hoy, Boni Joi, Dave Johnson, Phillis Levin, Philip Levine, Sharon Olds, and Alan Michael Parker – for your insight and invaluable advice.

Thank you to those who supported and contributed to this book, especially Victor Lunoki, Lucy I Ianna, Yvette Garcia, Jennifer Marosy, Kerry Mellor, Chris Poppe, Jim Sweeney, Stuart Wexler, and Neil Wiltshire.

Every map is a fiction. Every map offers choices.
It's even possible to choose something beautiful.

D.J. Waldie

Promenade

Over the sound of invisible cars
a woman whispered: *you are comforting
because you are dirty*. She promised

she had only felt this way
about one other river. Also dirty.
Also thoughtfully named

with a flawed sense of direction
in mind. For the third time
I said the prayer I use

when something proves the world
exists. Once for a man wiring fixtures
for stars. Once before the bodies

began to pile up. Blessed is the sick day.
Blessed are things that open
for no reason. Instead of fireworks

the air of geraniums. Neighbors
walking home to another light
to hunch over. Blessed is the strange

backyard that dwarfs us, the shoemaker
who tut-tuts our bitten heels.
Tomorrow I will suddenly think

of windowboxes and not know why.
Her dress was the shape of crickets. It said
I am the perfect shade of green.

ONE

Satellite Photos of Our Former Homes

(Legend)

From here you can see my hometown
is roughly heart-shaped
because that is how the filthy river bends:
Valentine heart not fist-heart
the sharp part pointing
at where Locust becomes Main
and the crooked line darkens
because that is where the river
scores the earth most deeply.

(28 Adamson)

When I have the dream about falling it happens on these stairs.
Though in the dream there are more of them and
it is not so much falling down as it is flying over.
The red dot is a spark in our bathroom wall.
After the first time your house burns nothing is ever the same.
Now you can see the future. The mind already sifts around its ashes.
There are no souvenirs. Instead, you remember everything
with its own small fire. Like a good Zoroastrian.
That way the burning is perpetual.
I have a cylinder of highway asphalt, some once-translucent shells:
pieces of cities I have loved more than this one
because they were not mine. Not in the way these streets are mine.
Because I might sleep through it next time.
Because it could happen while I am out. I am asking you
wherever you are: please save these things for me.

(229 H_____)

The street was called something
like Hayworth or Hawthorne, except it wasn't a word
you've heard before. We lived on the block between a tavern
and the funeral home: it was busy
between four and seven every day, between wakes.
The red dot is the candy store
I stole from the day I left for summer camp
where a girl named Tijuana
taught me how to speak in the third person.
Tijuana don't drink no milk
she would say every morning at breakfast.
That was the summer before the landlord
died in my mother's arms as his wife shouted
do something. People are always shouting do something
to my mother in the tone we use when there is
nothing to be done. His wife said nothing
for weeks after, except for his name.
Tijuana don't like where it came from.
I'd never thought of it that way before.
I'd never thought part of the self could be
pared away, becoming something
separate, with its own name.

(200 Mt. Pleasant)

This house is gone now: you are looking at a ghost house.
I like not being at the mercy of the real: the absence.
I like thinking there's this one dream everyone has:
it makes me feel more human. Last night I had the dream
about falling. And the night before that
the one where you hit the deer with your car.
It always runs into the woods: you never know
if it lived or died. Unless something breaks
you can't even tell it happened. The red dot near the rosebush is either
the top of my head or my grandmother's Pekingese.
I am seven years old: it is midday and I am
behaving myself. My dress remains clean
but I am about to scrape my knee. I'm watching ants drag
a monarch butterfly through the dirt: it takes hundreds of them.
I wonder if it will bleed. I wonder if these are the same anthills
my mother's brothers used to stick firecrackers into.
They said: *It's no worse than what happens when it rains.*
This house had a piano in the basement.
Right outside the bomb shelter. Around the corner
from the washing machine: it's amazing
what water can do. Maybe someday I will teach my-
self to be cruel. Maybe ants get used to it: the perpetual
building. But I am not yet imagining the future.
I am seven years old: certain that when the floods come
this will be the last house standing.

(45 Plaza)

In the middle of the map an egg balances
on a stretched out pentagon. Both are made of grass.
I lived here: on the egg's lefthand edge.
The red dot is a rooster.
One spring someone dropped a rooster
behind the fence around the egg. It had something
to do with Easter. For months I woke to the sound of it
crowing. I saw silos in my sleep.
I felt at home on my dream farm.
A lamb ran through the living room Christmas morning.
It was either the future or 1959. Either something I imagined
or something that happened to you. It's hard to tell.
The calves were newborn and blinking.
I spoke to them in the words I used
when I was closer to the ground.

Postcard

(Tyniec)

You said be sure to see the cows, and I saw the cows. They were not like ours. There was no tether, no bell. There were six of them, gathered in a sparsely flowered field. You can tell they remember winter. They are not sentimental. Perhaps that is what makes us American. If you come this way, bring small change. You will hear the cows before you see them. It is cool in the monastery where they chant the mass in Latin. I know now why we are the way we are. It came to me as I watched them, nudging each other at the trough they shared.

Take

Take this wedding dress.
The way it hangs from the clothesline
it could belong to anyone.
It could easily be

mistaken for a cloud. I was once
that white. I was underwater
with sun stabbing in at awkward angles
like luminous broken legs.

Like spider light. Two things are certain:
nothing smelled like flowers
and nothing hurt. Not even
when I hit the ground

trying to keep the water from pooling
off me. You set the garden on fire
and we watched it burn
as if it had nothing to do with us.

A rosebush startled, the pigeons
kept up their nodding and begging.
Later, the dog was replaced
by another with the same name

the same sad, jerking chain.
You were right when you said
a praying mantis is the one
sacred thing on this earth.

Take this dress. It's yours.
I would go barefoot and give a night

when all my poems are about him.
I would choose different instruments:

better a trumpet than the gutless
flute. Better the harp. This is how I say:
the heart is no constant thing. And you say:
remember that time I saved your life.

Watching the Girl

Today we begin to learn the slow lesson
of forgetting. In the future,
everyone you once loved will be reduced
to one essential thing: hair in the basin,
a beautiful back, more beautiful from a distance
and in street light. I will be the bread
improperly cut on a diagonal, the air in a finished
basement, or the song unfit for singing
unless we make the penguin a monkey,
leave out the dead dog. I will never be an antidote
for rain. Remember me this way:
making of my arm something like a wing.

The Lifespan of Birds

Now we feed the ducks
but call them swans. History tells us
the names of beautiful things

are easier to pronounce.
In this scene, the stream is called a river.
There are several balding trees

and one benevolent child
aiming for the skinniest bird.
His hand, the bread

always threatening to come loose.
Most things live longer in captivity.
If I were a swan and

he were a duck, we would fold
our heads into our wings, lower
thin membranes against the night.

In the story, it is winter
and the swallow should fly south
but does not. He says it remains

out of love. He says something
about tomorrow and breakfast
and seabirds. I am up all night

inventing a backstory for the albatross.
One without a lonely lifetime
never touching land. It is difficult

to make it both comforting
and true. So far, the albatross
remembers everything and lives in a poem.

The swallow will never catch cold.
Overnight, ducks will lengthen
their necks and grow pale.

September

For once clouds come to mark the day and one boy
tries to explain the sky with physics.
He will kneel this way for hours, weighted down
by pockets full of green glass and agate.
Because there is no wind the clouds persist
and the other boy knows he is being shown
a kind of mercy, as when a great force
hits something smaller but leaves it intact.
The trees are just as bright, just as near turning.
His street lifts the same way along the park,
but he cannot see the rest of the day
this small season was built around. From their hands
marbles fan across the sidewalk.
Most go where they are meant to
and the boy on his knees calls out the names
of obscure constellations. If he stares long enough,
he can torture patterns from the scattered glass:
first Carina, then the entire Argo Navis.
The other boy imagines living in a city built of clouds.
Every other green marble flies toward the grass.
Already birds are beginning to thin themselves out
and the blunt sound of helicopters
weaves less distinctly through a silence.
The grass is full of tiny eyes.
A patch of blue is forming as if a day can be replicated,
in all of its stillness, its clarity not of this earth.

A series of disconnected events

The earth moved closer and closer
to the sun, then began to turn away.
One man was captured on his front lawn.
Because he was first, we called him
the bellwether. He was blindfolded until
nothing had light. There were many words
but only one he understood.

Someone said there are guns hidden
on the moon if we need them.
Someone said: this is just like the time...
though it was nothing like that time at all.
The cameras were everywhere
so we could not touch, or sleep
or beg for our lives in peace.

When the floods came, they came without warning.
There were laments in every language
and the best were set to music.
Soon, every song sounded like something
from Ecclesiastes, the way *white amaurosis*
sounds like a flower, but isn't.

The blue persisted, without horizon.
One child held fast to a door, as other remnants
of fragile homes floated by him.
He was first to wash ashore.
When he spoke, he did not use his word for god.
He said: I cried for a long time. And then I was quiet.

It is quite possible (after all)

A morning spent staring at the ground.
No moon is scheduled, but you are sure it will happen.
Somewhere there is an ocean you are aware of
in only the vaguest way, persuading itself to shore.
The field and barn hold their respective shapes.

You can tell the plant by its flower
but its leaves are clearly oak. You want to give it a name.
The flower imagines itself a tree and you imagine
a children's story without a moral, resolving
that the protagonist must never sleep.

Against the barn, a botanist uses watercolor
to decipher green. Something significant is happening
in the corner where she was only mixing paint.
The spider is tentative and amused. With each shift
of its body, it invents a new equation.

The botanist says a fictional lake took shape
when she got distracted by the oak leaf hydrangea.
Now you know you were right about everything.
Green remains her nemesis. Call the painting *what if*.
Let the butterfly in the branches be a moth.

On Balance

In the beginning there are two of everything,
or one, roughly divided into equivalent parts:

the bicycle, the hourglass. The seesaw
and you in the air. The other end

not empty, but potentially empty
and you with so much to protect:

a pair of shoes, a pair of kidneys, and gravity
always pulling, pulling, always

demanding motion: the bicycle. The hourglass
and how the heart narrows.

Notice the sand, which is somehow
both inside and beneath you.

Notice whatever is down there
this time, holding you up.

In the beginning you believe in one thing
enough to pray for it: *stop up my heart,*

o god. Time always spilling and you
with just one small, resilient machine.

A bicycle, the beautiful symmetry
of one half repeating: *home before dark,*

home before dark.

TWO

The Horse Letters

(one)

The horses here are how you like them: indifferent
and showered in orchids: everything in flower
but the berries: so low to the ground: their leaves
do not suggest the storm: if you could see what comes crawling
over their little heart shapes: you would paint them
a less compelling color: I would know them
by the sound they make: today I was close enough
to see the iris open willingly and one bee
defer to another: new forms of chivalry
are invented each day: I, for one, have felt a hand
at the headboard: I have heard the sink scoured
in the middle of the night: sad instruments
sang me to sleep: lying down
we cannot help but resemble prey: the horses
are white: swinging their manes at lovelorn
stumbling cicadas: speaking of which:
I miss you: this is written
in the voice you use to read aloud: in total darkness
very quietly: in a shade of red
no one has seen before: not one thought
for that song: the unsteady mouth at the reed.

The Horse Letters

(two)

The hardest part is describing the sky: at dusk
we're covered in a color it cannot keep to itself:
today everything is purple: the grass
and the gardener's broadcloth shirt:
I remain green: my body
now a spool of vine: this time last year:
broken glass in a cylinder
aimed at trees: the horses too are resolute things
a master welder brought together from iron left behind:
they may be palominos but who can tell
what's under winged breastplates:
tea kettle feet for stomping out sorrow:
who can sum the parts of horses?
when the larger one rears up: is it fear
or threatening to show its clockwork heart?
you would know:
though the pieces are widely dispersed:
this is how the world will be some winter
in a snowstorm made of violets:
I am starting to believe in how the sky gets in us:
tinges our viscera the color of dusk:
a blueprint for what joy looks like: the pony
about to find its legs.

Postcard

(Los Angeles)

We did our best with the solution, sugar to crimson to water, but the birds of stunning heartbeat have gone out of season. Already dolphins shun the frigid coast. Every morning, ants flock and take form on the granite: today it was a map, defining the edges of what sweetness remains. I have come to see their consistency for what it is: a kind of love, shaming our fickle, pretty creatures. Though we nightly salt against it, nothing is shaped as this is shaped.

Poem Written on the Moon

After a long absence, the snow returned.
I had forgotten the last time
it fell so hard, how it erased the cars and trees
and we could no longer see the road
or where the holes were, just the soft
new shape of them.
Between the moment it stopped
and the moment the first animal
marched over, I thought:
this is what it must be like
to live on the moon. Imagine if it snowed
all the time, but without the falling.

From the moon I could see time
for what it really is: a relentless
spinning in place. Calibrated
to the fragile atmosphere,
I traversed the holes, the dark places
masquerading as seas.
Sea of Crisis, Sea of Cold. Lake of Joy.
By day the sky was a barcode
made of static. It made the sound of a dark room
populated with bees.
Night was like standing on a mirror:
the moon has no light of its own.

I asked you for another name
to call it by, something more specific.
Now there is nothing left to say
about the moon, but that it is beautiful.
It is cold and going nowhere.

Insomnia

Snow makes a white room of the garden, until there is no distinction. Night and the ceiling made from the same folded paper. The bed made of snow. This is what the honey locust would look like growing from the floorboards. If the candle shadowed its limbs and a moth flew in, against its will. Deer pause to lick walls made of salt. Legs meet fences in the dark. Nothing else touches. If I knew where green reposes I would go there. Here night is numbered and falling from the edges. It is hard not to think of their soft tongues, dissolving this room to nothing. I draw on your back the map of a country I have never seen, making of it something less familiar. All of it: the deer, the relentless spine, takes on aspects of architecture. Cold, white breath, the night is getting away from us. One of us must sleep.

Snow Machines, Astor Place

Briefly, the moon turns orange. A pigeon falls
    in the espaliered roses, seemingly from nowhere.
It is like that all week: I'm kicking leaves.
    I'm carrying a pumpkin. I think I have the answers
then I stumble on the outskirts of a movie set
    snowstorm. And as I search for a word
to modify the beauty of it all, a woman signifying
    preternatural pretends to shiver, pretends to love.
The truth is all around me. Here, actors play lovers
    setting fire to aphids. There, exterminators finish the insects
that daily plagued your kitchen. These events are distant,
    but simultaneous. Is it a sign?
The truth is, it was the ants' tenacity
    that meant something to me. Or was it the act
of washing them away and how useful I felt,
    hunched over their panic like an angel.
The script keeps changing and I become more familiar
    each day. This scene is called *snow machines,*
uma thurman and me. I played her once, another Halloween,
    another circle over my heart. Everyone knew who I was.
All of which implies connection, invites belief:
    She shivers. She loves. And this sudden January seems so sincere,
despite the white spheres, more beautiful broken apart.
    The truth is: this snow will not melt in my hands.
The truth is making me cold.
    I huddle under an awning with strangers.
We reach out our tongues, ignore the relentless humming.
    It means nothing.
Things just die sometimes. Birds, for example.

The Horse Letters

(three)

Lonesome charioteer: there is trouble with the horses.
In all this traffic, they see some things but not others
and do not respond to music. The gods were cruel today:
refusing to pass out the good wings, obscuring the pasture
with fog so they could not be followed.
Our souls began to starve. They sent a dream so universal
and imperfect it felt real. It hurt a little like something being
ripped away. In the end: one horse fell for the first he heard
breathing. The other is a thoughtful, reticent beast:
an apprentice to the meadow, looking upwards as birds do.

Ventriloquism

> *Propositions can be true or false only by being pictures of the reality.*
> - Ludwig Wittgenstein

This is a picture of my reality: in October, near the intersection
    of Beverly and N. Fairfax, stephanotis flowers

on a taverna patio, just like it must in summer, in Athens.
    At any given moment in Los Angeles

something is in bloom. And it is exhausting, this relentless
    insistence on beauty, on averting the inevitable pause

stop, end. Dinner has finished and we are on the sidewalk
    awaiting the slow valet. The shops are dark

obscured by gates. We can make out the contents
    of only one window: salt and pepper shakers

coupled, dressed in suits and veils: bride, groom, bride
    groom. Hundreds of them, as if it is not a miracle

surviving decades of everyday use, intact despite what surrounds us:
    precarious ceiling, defunct chandelier. Below, a marionette

sits alone on a toy piano. When headlights pass over, I swear
    his black eyes flash. Has it always been with us:

this tendency to mistake life-like for living?
    Daphne, Cyparissus: the human in us made wooden

we try to carve ourselves back out.
    The way the glass divides us is cruel somehow.

But what good would it do to reach under the surface,
    feeling for what strings it together, what causes it

pain? Backbone, fontanel: the places within us
      that cannot be touched. It recognizes something

I expect it to name. I know the hinge is worn. I know it sticks.
      But I want to hear the truth

out loud for once. Something from inside its small container
      of voices. The answer depends on what the heart is

fashioned from: metronome or mechanical bull. A simple machine
      that moves only back and forth. Logic, Reality: in his index

Wittgenstein lists everything that can be said. The rest
      we must pass over in silence. We may speak of necessity

but not need. And we may not speak of the heart,
      which should lie here, between *God* and *Hieroglyphic Writing*.

He means there are languages no one commands, limits
      to what the human hand can do. Philosophy, Los Angeles:

they are connected somehow, but tonight I cannot
      be contented by beautiful exteriors, by the distant, invisible

rhythm that may or may not beat underneath. Earlier he tells us:
      truth is a black dot on a white page, which I want

to believe, perhaps because the image is so clear, no moving parts
      and nothing to do with words. Black eyes,

you seem true to me. I will believe it if you point to your heart and
      say nothing. I will understand this to mean *I feel it everywhere*

but here.

The Horse Letters

(four)

Finally: the fences swung open
and the horses ran off. The hardest part

was knowing what to call the loss:
memory made their markings run together

forming one horse of a single color.
Years later, we were still trying to describe it:

maybe an Arabian, but less steadfast
and without the clean lines, made of wood

with an army inside, or an escaped racehorse.
You may know him: his name in all the papers,

his neck a wall of roses. This is how forgetting
happens: the sadness gets smaller, migrates.

Tell me: what was it in this empty palm that meant
so much? Where has it gone: my tether

sugarcube: clearly I am no expert.
between horses. Once the question

to me: feline is to cat as equine is to ___
answer seemed obvious.

es its bed in the barndoor's narrow sunlight
nds to a burden before knowing its weight.

Postcard

(Krakow)

I'm watching carriages negotiate corners the way I had been moving for months: like an exhausted palomino dragging tourists around the square, a hook in my head shaped like a hand. I know it's not the whip hand that makes horses shy but the one that strokes the mane. The voice saying: *look at my trick horse*. At night I brush her until she believes she is loved.

Cygnus

Sometimes you catch the attention of a god & get turned into a swan:
Perhaps you set yourself on fire.
Perhaps you were guilty of making too sweet a sound.
Once you wished sorrow would roll gently off.
Now the cold, immaculate wing: This is what prayer gets you.
The point is you're a swan now, or something shaped like a swan
& cannot remember what you were before.
Seagulls form battalions that dissolve & go idle.
Small fish tremble from the surface.
The carousel sings a paper boat to shipwreck.
You are no longer human, but not yet made of stars.
In myth, there is always a second chance
& someone always ruins it by looking back.
In one version, the same meddling god leaves a mirror lying on the riverbank:
Carelessness? Or spite.
In another, you are a bridge of magpies. Just for a night:
One night to pour out the year's entire longing.
Either way you find out what you are:

I can see myself now. I have gone white.
I am floating and nothing can touch me.

Nocturne: Shelter Island

The last ferry leaves and I watch it
become a dim light at pier's end, thinking
it does not matter to me as my rowboat
thuds the piling. And I would lie here awhile

but everything is moving forward.
The wind wishes it of all of us: ragged net
and towline, hurricane lamp. It urges us
off our hooks. An entire island out of season,

empty slips and every other mansion
abandoned. Only the ocean insisting on its sound.
In a bay window a green balloon bobs
toward the amber chandelier. A dead seagull,

a circle of claw prints around it in the sand.
Further on, a bouquet of rose stems, petals detached
by some blunt force, the bow: immaculate,
gathering back a short-lived joy.

We leave behind scenes others come upon and wonder
what happened. The bird becomes a god
the world forms around. Broken glass takes
the shape it once made as it lit the way back.

Bathymetry of Lake Michigan

The three black dogs in the water
are different versions of the same dog.

Each adores you in its own way.
Each is a dark cloud barely visible

through the fog. You say the lake
is infinite and I say it is the one

shaped like an ant, an insatiable ant
eating its way into the next lake.

Gulls relax around me until I am
made of gulls. The center cloud

becomes a mule, then a hamster
bunched up in the corner of its cage

then no animal we can recognize.
I can no longer see you as you were

approaching. The edge of Michigan
grows more and more invisible.

It is a convincing horizon, the kind
that conjures whales, breathing

beneath waves on the almost ocean.
I am inventing a way for us both

to be right. If we throw a jellyfish
in there, it will glow. If we look up

and say *rabbit*, together, out loud.

The Whole Is Greater

If you were the air you'd be blue and shaped like
        clouds
                shaped like birds
                          & I'd forget the science
of how one makes the storm &
                    one is a dark balloon
that warns of its coming. Before I knew
                        their true names
or could tell fair weather
                from stratus
                      from column rain
I was another animal
            the grass grew under
in the sun's uneven heating
                of the surface
                      of the earth.
Now these walls hold the sky & the birds
       become planes
                sharp-nosed & hovering
above their targets.
            Your colors run
eyes recede
       & limbs. If all of my animals were armless
they could not escape
              or touch me back
                      but with the open
wound of the mouth.
            And there would be no rain.
And I will call them

    duckclouds
        & you
            my demented horse
because I see in you
        a beautiful symmetry.

Organic machinery

To get an idea of the difference think of a rusted swingset: lambent from crying out the pain of its life: in this way we warn each other off the shoreline: take care what you rub up against: for example: you never know what seagulls will do next: trust me: there are nocturnes in their voices: I too dive for the invisible: I have blood on my mouth

You confess to longing in several species of water: salted soft loyal and falling: the earth is otherwise yellow flowers: we have seen this from great heights: we have emerged radiantly eroded: it is important to know what is beneath you: I think: I saw a starfish at your feet: I can tell you make the sweetest sound at the most inappropriate hour

THREE

Only one element of each kind

When the hummingbird stopped moving, the caretaker said: even in death, it's beautiful. We were inside a small poem about the heart

until the child beside him said: that was my second hummingbird, and we knew something important had been ruined. At night, insects mass

to form a disappointment you can see coming. Highway sixty-one runs too close to the greenhouse, frightening the turtles and there are not two of you: who is to blame?

For the still iridescent machine, we all thought the same perfect thought.

Billie Holiday

It snows the night he brings me violets
Clouds bloom a pale highway, strung with a bridge of violets

Phrases unfold in my throat like sharp paper animals
Falling from my mouth, the notes a plantation of violets

Bird's eye in a storm drain, arms of magnolia:
I am made of darker things than violets

He calls to me with violets and violets spring from faults
in the floor and my bones are a scaffold of violets

I sing to you with petals lying on my tongue
Violets for the gin glass, ruins spread with violets

Nancy Spungen

Being born blue is like holding the sky inside you:
it's the same trick of the eye: your mother whispers:
you are made of hyacinth & you try to speak the language
of flowers: imagine a tongue covered in pollen:
call the bees inside you but the bees will not come:
swallow sharp things: you bleed:
you fade: you learn the sky is not blue either:
nor is the earth as round as they said it was:
more apple than orange & you are more seed
than flower: not the flourishing but the heart:
its green shoot that will someday tear the earth:
the sky: benevolent lies: divots that have marred
your once-perfect world: the end written into
the beginning: red flowers spilling out of you:
the sky now above where it belongs:
a white sky filled with black wings & your heart
like the seed in a bird's mouth.

The Color and the Shape

Homesick palm trees line the road to the airport.
Planes come in carrying more things that will never leave.
In time, they too will become impossibly thin.
They will begin to sway, their pallor hidden under sunshine.
It is mercenary how things are chosen.
How they are plundered from the cold.
Florida is a perpetual summer of housecoats.
No strands of pearls, no snapdragons.
You play guitar by the shore, suspecting nothing.
There are memories of the sky as an overexposed photograph.
Of ex-husbands and sweaters. The warning of visibly waning breath.
Secretly, spheres grow in the body, black but orange
sized. The spaces they inhabit are random and hidden.
A distant winter smells like butter and onions.
Cedar closets full of china and candy and mink.
You recall knowing orange as a color between red
and yellow. Now it is inside you, getting larger.
If you dream, it is of hothouse flowers.
Seen from above, the state lingers in the shape of a lung.

Eve

If the cold were a fist it would come down
    common over you and the world
so that one thing could not be told
    from another. It would hurt
if you were tangled naked
    and longing for birdsong. Each day
more muffled than the last and you
    shrouded in wool, try to keep snow
from falling inside you. The ground dreams
    itself the color red and the sky
tells an elaborate, whispered lie.
    It would hurt like secrets
kept from you in your own trees:
    a sudden clutch of robins
a premonition of summer thunder
    shaking sugar from pears. And you
will pull the fruit down, ask the leaf
    what will make it shiver
just to hear it say

    touch me, slowly, here.

Map of Trees

So far, there is the corner of Reservoir
and Brook, what is either
a praying mantis
or a small plane on the sidewalk.
The peach tree can be anywhere.
You have the pen.
The wind can be made of color and your breath
is the fragile, quickening
cloud, but you are not the peach tree.
You only dug the hole, all at once
before something came to fill it.
The emaciated stray
or the rain.
In the vicinity of June, you dug the hole,
which does not make you the peach tree
or the clothesline or anything children hang hope on.
You are the oak.
No one forgets where the oak was
or how it came down, piece by piece,
insisting. You have the pen
and I have the spoon and comb,
but we are not the sarvis blossoms.
No one gets to be the blossoms
that fall all at once and somehow
never bruise. No one gets to be
the scaffold of leaves.

Lazarus

I slept surrounded by moths.
        I could feel them, moth breath
soundlessly eating away
        at the wool on my eyes.

Then I was awake, walking by a low tree,
        red birds rushing its branches.
Recent snow made everything familiar.
        A woman spoke a name to me:

Mary. Then the beekeeper's silver clothes.
        Then the eloquent god she bathed
to wake me. I forgave the limb
        I once stepped out on

for not breaking and my heart,
        ticking toward a second death.
Seeing, I knew the names of things
        but not the trouble in them.

Only the living remember that way.

I knew the table and chairs, the order
        of still life: first willows,
then wine. Then a flying thing
        grounded for the feast.

If the Soul Has a Shape

It is not the outline of the body
as it forms an algorithm
for setting itself on fire

or the mind composing an ode
unaware that it is badly hurt.

If the soul has a shape
it holds water. It is an aquarium
full of strangely conscious fish.

Nothing happens for days.

The body aches with indifference.
The mind forms a single phrase

how audible the water

and the wet little world
with no wind inside
just glows.

What moves the soul
cannot be proven
because no one has ever seen one.

There are days you have nothing
to show for. There are days
you go on existing
though the room seems empty.

The mind takes a hard look

at the body's diminishing

and remembers the soul
as a pristine thing
of no substance.

Now it has shape and breath
and light inside.

Now it is the one thing
that makes a sound.

What the soul wants is silence
but a small machine
carrying on in the background
speaks of some unfinished business.

It speaks of the shipwreck
in the corner

and fat pink fish are gaping
feed me, feed me

but you do not touch the glass.

Diane Arbus

How to give a name to what exists now only as fragments:
bus stop, brown house, blonde nurse whose favorite phrase was
everyone dances in heaven. Soup spoon, small plane

humming overhead and my grandfather saying, that's what I
always wanted to do, then retreating to the strange intermediate
he lived in, where he smelled the pig farms the Meadowlands

used to be, where it was time to pour molasses over grain
bought from the brewery, and play Viennese waltzes to calm
his cows for milking, the whole time listening for planes

on their way from Newark or Teterboro. Just to fix them, he said.
Not even to fly. I used to think heaven was a lie we told the dying,
another cloudy abstract not for us to decipher. It was not there

in the fields of New Jersey that Arbus said: *I seem to have discovered
sunlight.* The crop in her field was people, *the strangest combination,*
she wrote, *of grownup and child I have ever seen.* Parading on Easter

and Halloween, wearing masks they made themselves.
Rolling on the grass, in the aftermath of a somersault. Clasping
their handbags, each other, an apple, trying to save something

for later. It was weeks after, the images still forming, when she knew
she had seen the faces we are all making inside. Underneath we are
pure terror and joy. We are Anne Frank and Bob Dylan, exhausted

starlets, all of us, superheroes, confused and wondering *was I
the only one born?* That must be what heaven is: an absence of worry
about not knowing, not being more. Mostly we are alone in a field

with a storm blurring the background, a new season bearing down,
everything and nothing changing. Sometimes, the body goes on
after the work is finished. More often, so much gets left undone.

We have never danced together, half-sleep, hipbone carving
your side, the wing of a tiny plane, trying to fly out of you.

Soteriology

Across the street, little boys strike a horse-
shaped piñata, and you imagine
which seam it will break along. The angle
of impact. What shape its scattering will take
on the ground. You know every day is your
birthday
and the party is always disappointing.
Every town is your hometown, every
building
the house you grew up in, its aluminum,
shag carpets and nightmares about falling,
for what seemed like forever, down the
stairs.
You think of winters in Utah. The smell of
Old Spice in the elevator. Your secretary's
story about her turtle winning a blue ribbon
at the state fair. And the last episode of *St.
Elsewhere*
when the autistic child shakes the city
inside his snowglobe to sudden weather
and the real city turns white for him,
the universe his own invention, solid in his
hands
snow falling, the boy thinking: *This world is
plastic
this world is mine.* This is the fourteenth
floor. You are called in sick from work
with your tie undone. These are the facts,
and there is comfort in them. Real horses
pull lovers toward the natural history

museum. Even they seem so small from here, like those green plastic combat horses, hardened into regal positions.
You remember learning every horse must be broken.
Every horse is born new and fierce. It's true: life flashes, but not the whole life, just images on a theme. Another window, another man busying his hands away thinking: *somewhere else*
somewhere else. There are cities you've never seen, where effortlessly bilingual shopgirls sell color-coded thrift. There are children building animals out of snow.
There is something on the other side of this moment, in which I am speaking to you from the future:
you there with the world in your hands: its racetracks and unfinished cathedrals, its airport service roads, desolate but lined with daffodils
grounding themselves on some strange asphalt.

The Naming of Things

There's a bird here so ubiquitous I've begun to think of it
as the Mexican house sparrow. Somehow I can tell
it's a roadrunner, a bird I've only seen in cartoons.
One summer at Wyeth's house there was a bird marked
like one of those skeleton suits they sell on Halloween.
I still call it *skeleton bird*. I'm only heeding Whitman
who urges an ignorance of nature, to preserve wonder.
A certain free margin, he calls it. A blankness. Yesterday
at the nursery my mother named eleven kinds
of lavender, deciding which would go better between
crepe myrtle and wisteria. I tried to save them
in the sound of her voice, for later.
But my brain holds only geranium, marigold,
begonia: botany of suburban America, all borders
and primary colors. There are 1,500 species of begonia
including the one my grandfather set in concrete
planters every spring, half red, half white, like the Polish flag.
Last night I stood in wet sand holding a lantern
and hundreds of infant turtles ran toward my light
anonymous as stars rained into the sea. Can you feel it?
How I'm keeping everything alive, omitting the gull
on the shore road, bent into a star, and the butterfly
caught in a windshield wiper, blue wings folded perfectly
in half, fluttering as if it might, at any moment
fly off.

Elliott Smith

Henry Gray can tell you the depth and breadth and height of the heart, but not how many hours until someone comes home to you. *The rhythmical action of the heart*, he wrote, *is muscular in origin— that is to say, the heart* moves itself and nerves have no say in it. Snow on your skin can be felt. A choke chain, pricks of poison, the dimensions of the living room when empty can be felt. All of it unnecessary to the movement of your heart. During times of rest, *the whole heart is relaxed.* If given the chance. If the bones of the hand do not articulate precisely as asked. If it ever becomes safe to stop hiding the knives. *During life, there is no vacant space.* Something for every cage, the carve of ribs, a lovely fist enclosing. This is the architecture of your heart.

FOUR

...And We Shall All Be Clean

I came this far to wash the smell out of my clothes. We go sightseeing
at three in the morning, when there are no lines and immense, unseen
seals cry from the wharf: afraid of the dark, or mourning
an undefined loss. Meteors shower from the radiant. Someone explains
Alaskan currents and the far reach of frigid water. Now the Pacific
is useless to me. Last night I called home to cancel Thanksgiving.
I said things like: *San Francisco is saving my life.* I've come to depend on
houses painted to match the hibiscus and the emptiness of
laundromats on weekdays. Time divides into seven-minute intervals.
Four heat settings are available. I put myself in charge of the color
blue, ponder the universal implications of turning the dial
to *normal*. I don't know what permanent press is or why seals
beach themselves on rotting piers. It's enough to make me pray,
the small mysteries that are left to me, white block letters
I can believe in, and clean underwear in case of accident.

The Damascus Encyclopedia

(Circle)

No pond is ever square and for good reason: we believe in the shapes we have lived with for so long. We know bodies made of water are elliptical, temporary. Rain angles and hits the perimeter. We circle, our frequent pausing a symptom of never knowing when to stop. The linear means nothing here, where our kind of waiting is the same kind endured by tadpoles or peonies: waiting for the true faces of things to emerge, knowing it will occur in the form of a burst and we will miss it, either sleeping or in the sitting room near the wood stove and depression glass ashtray. Near the phone. Listen. Several new species sing or cry or beg one another for some small mercy. It's impossible to tell. In a world without end, what will come of all this?

(Tadpole)

Midsummer and the body, between two states, becomes a stranger to itself. The sun pierces last season's soft, dull leaves. Of all the various shades of green, we have settled on this one, the one immune to weather. A half-fish widens as new lungs grow inside. It has begun peering above the surface. And the fully-evolved stare back, helpless like butterflies remembering the canyons they came from, the dark that bred their markings. Now it resides in the hand, a waterlogged chrysalis, wetly blinking as limbs begin to sprout. It wishes back another way of breathing, one that leaves less exposed. There is always something to be done, of course: lure, net, a push to shore will make it otherwise. Too clearly is how we see it coming: how it will reach, then run.

(Ice)

The ice floating in our pitcher is the same as a glacier, but on a smaller scale. In Antarctica, scientists monitor the songs ice makes as it breaks away, back to the water it came from. What it wants is a return to the beginning. It wants another chance. They say that's how you can tell an iceberg from an earthquake, by the way water moves inside. It sounds like a double string quartet. It sounds like bees, or the score to a horror film that leaves one last girl alive to tell the story. But what can a song tell us of absence? Of an engagement broken before the dress was bought, or why photographs remain but the guns are gone. After dinner, Peggy Lee on the radio singing *is that all there is?* one of us burns the trash, while the other sits on a tree stump, watching for bears.

(Salt)

Life goes on, and by life we mean merely some movement of elements in combination. We know what we are made of: carbon and iron. Heart in a sack, hundreds of bones. All of it floating, tethered by bonds tiny and translucent. There is a science to attachment, to need. The elements of salt seek one another, their movement willful, almost human. Neither can exist alone. Remember limping across the field, skin broken, bee writhing, its little knife half inside? A bee would rather die than go on, defenseless. But in this brackish pond a body, half-immersed, will not dissolve. Water moves through our fractures, singing. We learned this as children: to brave the sting. What hurts the wound will heal it.

(Script)

In the end the screen goes dark, then fills with words and music. The words are names of people we do not know, and the song sounds familiar because it was playing during the scene entitled *ice rink with winter laughter*. We love the part when snow has just covered filthy rooftops. We hate the part where someone leaves. When at last the man and woman stop speaking, even the music is about silence, how words echo and fail. Years pass. They always meet again, always by chance: at the protest, or outside the concert hall. We have seen it all before, from the image of two hands, holding in the cold, to their sad goodbyes on the sidewalk. Why turn back now? Why watch again and pray for a different ending?

(Field)

Only one thing is clear at the outset and that is how it will all end up. If a young man's first words are: *I want it to be different*, we know the same grief will repeat itself, and that he will make it so. Just as when the first person ever to enter a drive-in said: what a strange and wonderful idea, it foretold the day the screen would come down. And not just the faces but the sound, not just the music but the earth it came from. The cornfield around it died in that quiet. Birds assumed their goodbye formation, then made the sound that means: we are never to return. Now the sky is so empty it seems newly born. Meaning there is finally an excess of light. Insects at work in the allium, its long stems tangled in our beautiful useless scarecrows.

Postcard

(from a train)

The shore is full of rowboats, frozen horizontal into this season's last snow. Everything else has come loose: pool ladder, black caboose, strand of birds. Ice: blue and white and broken, like the surface of earth seen from space. Lawnmower, bright yellow crane. Covered bridge. Another. Another. Stories spelled out in metal and weather. I'm trying to decipher the language of silos, the glittery abstract letters made of geese.

Letter to Colin Concerning the Birds of Poland

The swallows wrap around St. Mary's the way they will
in the poem you write this morning in Paris over coffee and
smuggled clementines.
                       But I cannot hear them,
so I listen to consonants curl around one another
the way they did when I was child, head in wing, and draw
the birdhouse I saw yesterday in the birch trees.
                                          There was
an excess of starlings. A couple walked by and one said
to the other
          *I wonder if there were so many birds here
then*, and I felt ashamed for knowing, for being able to see them
pecking in dandelion and clover growing in small patches of grass
around the sewers of a terrible suburb.

                                   We arrived late
to the salt mines, too late to hear the tour in English,
so we tried to think of songs with salt in the lyrics, coming up empty
until Jim said,
              Well, it's sugar for sugar and salt for salt,
whatever that means.
                      It's a game I always win, but not today.
Today I was thinking of the men down there in the dark, carving
chandeliers and statues, and when the guide turned her back,
I ran my tongue along the wall, to taste a world made
with picks and axes.

                    Now the trumpeter
sounds the hour from his little window, and the swallows ebb
for the moment.
                  You left before saying why they act this way.
It is foreign to me, the idea of return, like another world

where things that have gone don't stay gone.

                                            I wanted to point
at the birdhouse and say
                  see how old the wood looks, or tell them the story
of how, in another prison, Messiaen heard black birds awakening
in the trees and began to imagine freedom.
                                     How he forced
the instruments he had together – the clarinet, cello and violin
of other inmates – to form the trumpet of the seventh angel,
the one who sounded the mystery of god.
                                The birds, he wrote,
are the opposite to time.
                  It seems like a small thing, but it means everything
that someone troubled himself to build a birdhouse, and someone
needs to believe it happened.

                    In a few days
I will stand near the Vltava as a man in the castle pulls a giant lever
and thousands of windows go dark at once, just as a star falls,
a star the river won't reflect.
                            You might say it is farther than it seems,
or that what you're up against makes things visible,
as you sit at a painted table, charting the tides around an island in France,
making sure the water brushes Anna's ankles just so.

I leave the swallows to you. I place them in your hand,
place their song in the palm of your hand, and we will work
with what we have—
                  scavenging slabs of wood, forcing music
from the boxes we live in—
                          and wring the eternal from our brief transit.

Postcard

(Montreal)

I'm in a scene from a Piaf film, snow floating over the iron spiral staircase, an invisible French woman singing "Il Faut du Temps au Temps." I know what you'll think if I say the snow looks like miniature angels, but it does. Little white dresses and wings. Happy birthday. My favorite photograph is of you looking back at me from the front seat of Stephanie's blue Hyundai. It's early spring, the Forked River rest stop. We are on our way to Ocean City to chase birds on an empty beach with a borrowed dog, and we know we will never grow old.

Postcard

(Prague)

On the fourth of July, I was lost in a cherry orchard near the world's largest metronome. It points the way to the museum of miniatures, where the Eiffel Tower stands inside a wild plum stone. A stranger kissed me between rosebush and riverbank. He found the button at the small of my back that makes stars fall. I have stopped wishing for something specific and enduring. I cannot tell if the city reflected in the river is still the city, or another version of where we are.

Bronze with Rabbits

Before I left my horoscope said something profound
but I only remember the words *freedom* and *alone*.
Between then and now was the moment
the plane hesitates, quiets its engines, rethinking the air.
You know this moment. It happens just before
it comes to you, through the smallest of windows
that we all live on top of one another
and have more baseball fields than necessary.
If each of us has our own equation, it's the time value
of solitude, subtracted by the bad dream
that recurred constantly in childhood, then disappeared
refusing to be summoned back. Last night
I dreamed I was a prime number. Indivisible.
There are nine rabbits at the base of this statue
but you can only see five from here.
Above, Peter Pan rounds his arm as if looking
for someone to dance with. A pride of fairies
whispers up at him: *grow. It's time to multiply.*
Here no one asks how you are. Today I feel celebratory
though it is not my birthday. I know this because it is warm
and I am not someone who would travel this far
on her birthday, depriving her mother of the chance to call
too early to say: *today I remembered the day you were born.*
Perhaps it is being on foreign time. Perhaps it's because
today I saw our city from a great height
as if it were that miniature village on PBS, the one
with tiny carnival rides, and it reminded me of being a child
though my backyard never had a Ferris wheel.
It is late where you are, or early. I'm watching
a pair of mute swans outmaneuver a flock of geese.
I want to tell you how I am: I am wondering
if rain is expected there, and whether the cats have caught
the waterbug that was keeping you up.

Chicken

Outside the Mexican carwash, Mayan children
thread gaps in cinderblock, and a chicken
crosses the road. I'm inside a riddle
about the obvious, watching a chicken
jerked along by the sound of its own alarm.
In Illinois, Amy still can't walk on the foot
that shattered with her windshield.
Amy's favorite word is chicken.
She can't say it without smiling: *Chicken*.
I ride that way too: heel against dashboard
foot arching over its reflection as cornfield
becomes wheat field becomes cattle becomes
Michigan, billboards passing from sight
the moment you can finally make them out,
thinking: *this is the world as it is,*
abstract and temporary, everything but this foot, this
body that carries me forward.
These children are not actual Mayans,
the ones who prayed for rain by painting men
the color of sky, then sending arrows
into their hearts. They cannot tell us
if the winged figure hanging upside down
over the temple of the descending god represents
a setting sun, or the dream of unmediated flight.
Or, as our guide said with such certainty: a honeybee,
grafting narrative to image, forcing it
to make sense in the logic of another time.
Sometimes one story becomes your only story:
This is the story of an intersection.
This is about the time you couldn't say your own name.
Inertia drives limb through image of limb.
A chicken crosses a road to eat from the neighbor's yard.

It crosses back when the rooster rears up in warning.
Now it is a fable of our common trajectory,
every step a response to need and fear.
Amy says she saw God in the emergency room,
holding her foot like a piece of raw meat,
mark of airbag and rearview mirror, the broken rib
that spared her heart.

Leaving Barcelona

On the fourth day, we crush the grapes ourselves. Orchard keepers shout directions, as if there is more than one way to march wine into being. The street names byzantine with consonants, we will never find our way on high school Spanish, drunken ankles.

Montserrat requires French and a monorail through yellow rocks. Caves that get so dark this time of year. Palm Sunday at the monastery giftshop: reproduction black madonnas and last chance conversions for the never baptized.

They sell honey sweeter, the legend goes, for having been reaped in silence.

Language is a strange religion when you do not have the words. It becomes exhausting to contemplate travel in space, where moons have moons and none of them have the same word for *umbrella*.

Who will write the phrasebook for the Pleiades? Who will order dinner so we do not starve?

If we have learned anything, it's that the best prayers are wordless, like packing while someone else sleeps. Intimacy in the body's comprehension. Knowing which clothes are unworn. Being able to say, without hesitation: nothing under the bed is ours.

This mirror does not show the space between things, but it came with the room. We are lost, yet we resist screaming. A single word can sour the harvest. It is a test of faith, to bolt up in bed and mouth the words slowly:

Take me to the cloister hive. Take me to the quiet bees.

Notes

The opening epigraph is from D.J. Waldie's *Holy Land*.

In "Elliott Smith," the italicized text is from *Gray's Anatomy* by Henry Gray.

The titles "A series of disconnected events," "It is quite possible (after all)," "Organic machinery," and "Only one element of each kind" are part of *Oblique Strategies* by Brian Eno and Peter Schmidt.

"Organic machinery" was inspired by "Crescent," by C.D. Wright.

The final line of "A series of disconnected events" is taken from words spoken by Lachie Searle, a survivor of the 2005 tsunami in Phuket.

In "Letter to Colin Concerning the Birds of Poland," the italicized lyric is from Bob Dylan's "Down in the Flood." This poem also references Olivier Messiaen's *Quatuor pour la Fin de Temps*.

"The Horse Letters (three)" was inspired by and incorporates phrases from Plato's *Phaedrus*, translated by Tom Griffith.

"Ventriloquism" begins with an epigraph from Ludwig Wittgenstein's *Tractatus Logico-Philosophicus*.

The italicized lines in "Diane Arbus" are from her journals. The poem references the series of photographs taken by Arbus at various group homes for the developmentally disabled in New Jersey.